Meeting special needs

a practical guide to support children with dyspraxia

by Mary Mountstephen

Note on Terms used in the book

Throughout this book the term practitioners is used to include all play workers, child minders and childcare workers.

The term 'setting' applies to wherever the play/childcare takes place.

The terms 'parent' or 'carer' are used interchangeably throughout this book

Although boys appear to be more prone to diagnosis for dyspraxia, the terms 'he', 'she', 'his' and 'hers' are used interchangeably.

Dyspraxia: Dyspraxia is generally recognised to be an impairment or immaturity of the organisation of movement. Associated with this may be problems of language, perception and thought (The Dyspraxia Foundation).

Neuro-Developmental Delay: The term Neuro-Developmental Delay (NDD) describes the omission or arrest of a stage of early development. Every normal, full-term baby is born with a set of primitive or survival reflexes that are inhibited or controlled by higher centres in the brain during the first year of life. If these are not inhibited at the correct time, they remain active in the body and can interfere with balance, motor control, eye functioning, eye-hand coordination and perceptual skills. They can result in behavioural symptoms such as frustration, hyperactivity and hypersensitivity, and failure to match performance to ability.

Motor skills: This refers to the actions that involve the movement of muscles in the body.

Gross motor skills: This refers to the larger movements of arms, legs, feet, or the entire body (crawling, running, and jumping)

Fine motor skills: This refers to smaller actions, such as grasping an object between the thumb and a finger, using scissors and cutlery.

www.practicalpreschoolbooks.com

Published by Practical Pre-School Books
St Jude's Church, Dulwich Road, Herne Hill, London, SE24 0PB Tel. 020 7738 5454
© MA Education 2010 www.practicalpreschoolbooks.com

Meeting special needs: a practical guide to support children with dyspraxia ISBN: 978-1-904-575-95-5

Contents

Introduction

Children who do not enjoy and achieve in their learning may, at some point, cease to engage with the learning process. When children are no longer motivated to want to learn this can, in the short term, lead to disruptive behaviour, even exclusion, and in the long-term will have an effect on their ability to achieve their full potential.

When a child seems to be falling behind others in their rate of early development, this can be a cause for worry and concern at home, at play and in early years' settings. In the pre-school setting, you may be working with a child who has problems with their movement, social interaction or play skills and you may be looking for reasons to explain this, and for advice on what you can do and how you can support both the child and his family.

Are you concerned about a child you know and observe who has a persistent combination or cluster of the difficulties below?

- Seems clumsy and bumps into others

- Stands too close to others or knocks over objects

- Is easily confused about finding their way

- Struggles with handling toys, balls etc

- Messy eater, often spilling things

- Poor concentration and abandons activities quickly

- Speech may be unclear or muddled with associated frustration

- Squinting, rubbing eyes, eyes running

- There is a mismatch between their innate skills and their fine and gross motor skills

- Prolonged behaviour problems such as extreme frustration, low self-esteem, social avoidance, fidgety and easily distracted

- Sometimes associated immune system weaknesses which can result in allergies, eczema, glue ear or year-round hay fever

Parents may be told that their child, who seems to be delayed in their development according to developmental milestones, will usually catch up in their own time. This is true in some cases; but we know that not every child moves forward at the same pace, or demonstrates new skills at the same time or rate as other children around them.

Development may be more advanced in some areas than others, and this can be confusing when trying to establish if there really is a problem. However, when a child seems to have a cluster of on-going challenges which are affecting their day to day living, steps need to be taken. It becomes increasingly important to identify the areas which are most in need of targeted support and to put into place strategies to support firm foundations for learning and living.

Helping Rosie

Rosie is four year's old and attends a Foundation Stage Unit. She has no diagnosis of dyspraxia, but there are concerns about how she is developing.

An adult might say:
'Rosie just can't stay on her chair and she's got more paint on her than on the paper!'

Rosie might say:
'Nobody wants to play with me'.

Her parent says:
'She's so slow, I still have to get her dressed or we'd never get here'.

The focus of this book is on helping you to identify what it is that Rosie, is finding hard to do and then using your observations and discussions to find ways of supporting her so that she can flourish and thrive to the best of her ability. If Rosie can be prevented from experiencing repeated failure, she is more likely to develop resilience and the self-confidence to try new activities. We know that the early years are a very important time for physical, emotional, intellectual and social development and those positive and negative experiences can have a profound influence on later learning and development. The earlier you can spot areas for concern and then intervene, the better the long-term prospects will be.

This book recognizes that children may have problems and difficulties but it also says that you can do something about it, not just wait in hope for change. Reading this book may be the first step you take in learning more about the importance of early identification of movement difficulties how they can be addressed.

Movement difficulties can be identified early; indeed they may be one of the first signs that extra support is required. And if identification is early, help, intervention, remediation, call it what you will, can be early too. (Macintyre, *Dyspraxia in the Early Years*, 2009)

If these difficulties are not addressed early, the child faces even more challenges when they start to write, maintain concentration, participate in physical activities as part of a group and organize themselves independently.

A problem which arises is the multiplicity of labels to describe difficulties of this type reflects the lack of agreement among professionals as to the specific causes and indicators or motor impairment. This can cause confusion for carers and others who are in contact with the child as there is such variability in the symptoms. Historically, many professionals have held the belief that developmental coordination problems may be outgrown as the children reach adolescence or adulthood. However, this is often not the case. While many clumsy children appear less affected as they become older, this is most likely the result of learning to adapt to their difficulties as well as learning to avoid situations where they have already experienced anxiety, frustration or failure.

As a professional, you may feel you need appropriate training and specialist advice on how to differentiate for Rosie and how to include her in activities. Can you make sure that Rosie has successful experiences, and what can you do if you feel that she is not making adequate progress? This book is not intended to cover all aspects of this complex disorder, but I do hope it will give you a greater understanding of the condition, as well as offering guidelines for support and signposts to further reading, professional development and useful resources.

I am passionate about the role of movement and developmental movement programmes in particular, and I make no excuse for the emphasis on this throughout the book. Movement is a child's first language. It is the means by which children come to understand the world around them. It is the basis of communication, language, sensory integration, learning and living (Goddard Blythe, S. 2008: What Babies and Children Really Need).

Three Children: Three Stories

Three children will appear in the book to illustrate particular points. The age range extends beyond the early years in order to present a wider perspective of the implications of dyspraxia.

Callum attends a Day Nursery and is three years old.

Rosie is four years old and attends a Foundation Stage Unit.

Liam is eight years old and attends a primary school. Before starting school, he attended a Day Nursery.

A Word of Caution

Not every child who shows signs of the difficulties or delays above will have dyspraxia: some children will make up their progress, although more slowly than others. It is when there is a persistent cluster of difficulties observed over a period of time that further investigation needs to take place.

Some facts about Dyspraxia

- It has been suggested that up to 10% of the total population may have dyspraxia, although a number of different figures are quoted.

- Risk factors that affect dyspraxia may include premature birth, prolonged pregnancy, problems around the birth process, or a family history of dyspraxia. The possibility of a link between premature birth or complications at birth, and the development of dyspraxia has been the focus of much debate.

- Dyspraxia appears to be four times more common in boys than girls. That is to say that boys are four times more likely to be referred for assessment. There is a suggestion that girls tend to be more precise in their fine motor activities while boys are faster and less accurate. This is often observed in pre-school children where boys often prefer gross motor play.

- Some different types of dyspraxia have been identified including Verbal Dyspraxia, Oral Dyspraxia, and Motor Dyspraxia. There is more information about these in the next section.

- Children with dyspraxia usually look physically normal, and dyspraxia is not acquired through accident or illness. It cannot be cured, but children can learn to cope better with some of the things they find hard to do.

- Dyspraxia can affect children mildly, or to a much more significant degree in that it gets in the way of positive and successful living and learning. Up to 50% of the most severely affected children will continue to have problems as adults. Dyspraxic children lack fluency even when basic movement skills have been mastered and they have difficulty adapting skills to different situations.

- Dyspraxia, Developmental Coordination Disorder (DCD) and Perceptual Motor Dysfunction are all terms used to describe children who may in the past have been called 'clumsy'. These conditions are found in children with normal or above normal intelligence and can lead to frustration, a sense of failure and low self-esteem if not addressed.

- In the UK, dyspraxia tends to be used more generally as the main term for coordination disorders although technically, Developmental Coordination Disorder (DCD) is the umbrella description used, with dyspraxia as one profile in this range of conditions.

- Dyspraxia is one of a group of Specific Learning Difficulties (SpLD) and there is often an overlap between dyspraxia and these neuro-developmental disorders:

    - Dyslexia : difficulties with learning to read and spell
    - Dyspraxia: difficulties in planning and the automatic organization of movement
    - Dyscalculia: difficulties associated with understanding mathematical concepts
    - Dysgraphia: difficulties with writing activities

- There are also often links between dyspraxia and other disorders such as Attention Deficit Hyperactivity Disorder (ADHD) and Autistic Spectrum Disorders (ASD).

- In a recent survey of 50 children with a diagnosis of dyspraxia undertaken by the Dyscovery Centre at the University of Wales, only 14% had dyspraxia as a single disorder, while the rest had dyslexia, ADHD, or combinations of these difficulties. Children who have a diagnosis of dyspraxia may also have an overlap with one or more of the conditions above, and are at risk of problems in learning, attention and social functioning. If you have one difficulty, you are likely to have more than one difficulty.

- Children with movement difficulties are often easily distracted and fidgety.

- Early intervention can help prevent frustration, anxiety and low self-esteem.

Three Main Types of Dyspraxia

Oral Dyspraxia

Speech requires many complex movements involving the tongue, lips, jaw and other structures. As a result, many children who have coordination problems have difficulties in coordinating speech and other activities involving the mouth and its structures.

Oral dyspraxia relates to difficulties with planning and carrying out non-speech sounds such as blowing, sucking, as well as tongue or lip movements. This may have an effect on speech and/or swallowing skills. There may be dribbling, difficulties eating, licking an ice-cream, or showing a preference for certain textures of food.

You may observe a child having difficulty imitating funny faces, sticking out their tongue, copying a rounded shape of the mouth or a limited ability to show their emotions in facial expression. It may also affect individual sequences of movements, such as moving the tongue quickly from side to side.

Verbal Dyspraxia

This is a speech disorder that affects the planning, sequencing and execution of movements for making speech sounds. The cause of verbal dyspraxia is not known but there is some evidence of a family tendency towards speech and language problems and with skilled professional intervention, most children should end up with clear, intelligible speech. (Wolverhampton City NHS: *Speech and Language Therapy: Verbal Dyspraxia Information Leaflet for Parents and Teachers*. See reference section for contact details).

Children with verbal dyspraxia may have speech which is hard to understand because they are having difficulties in making and coordinating the precise movements of the speech muscles necessary for clear speech. There is no damage though to the muscles or nerves. Children may simplify words: e.g. 'bur' for 'burger', or they may muddle up the order of sounds in a word. They may also pronounce the same word inconsistently.

You may observe them moving their tongue and lips around as they try to work out how to make a sound and they may use gestures to help them express what they want to convey.

The important thing is that the child knows what he wants to say but persistently makes speech errors which are not usually made at his/her age. As a result, they may come to avoid speaking and so don't get the practice they need.

Motor Dyspraxia

This term relates to difficulty in planning, sequencing and carrying out sequences of movements in a smooth and coordinated way under good control. It is related to voluntary control of age appropriate skills. This can have an impact on many areas of learning and generalizing, so that a skill learnt in one context can easily be transferred to another.

When Callum explores a new toy, he initially gains sensory information about how it feels, looks and smells. In order to do this, the motor planning area of the brain must work out and plan which arm and leg muscles to move and how Callum can maintain balance whilst the sequence is carried out. Although Callum is of average intelligence, he may behave immaturely and it will take him longer than some other children to manipulate the toy effectively.

How to Identify Difficulties

Our society has moved babies into buggies and other 'containers' which limit their early movement experiences which strengthen muscles, hearts and lungs as well as their awareness of balance and where they are in space. We have also moved older children indoors (or they have moved themselves!) as they become less physically active and more drawn to social interaction via other means.

At birth a baby is unable to move voluntarily, yet by the end of the second year of life, the infant has developed a wide range of fundamental movement skills which will form the foundation for more complex skills. The human nervous system is immature at the time of birth and a number of factors will have an impact on the child's rate and quality of development such as genetic or inherited aspects as well as cultural, lifestyle and environmental elements.

For successful motor learning, the child needs frequent opportunities to physically explore surroundings so

that they develop an appreciation and awareness of being active in a natural way. However, there is growing evidence that many young babies are not getting enough time on their tummy throughout the day when they are awake and supervised.

We have seen first-hand what the lack of tummy time can mean for a baby: delays in developmental, cognitive, and organizational skills, eye-tracing problems, behavioural issues, to name some complications. (Towne Jennings, American Physical Therapy Association website)

While putting infants to sleep on their backs is still seen as vitally important in reducing infant deaths, many therapists believe that there should be more education for parents of the benefits of bringing babies out of infant carriers, that double as car seats, and onto the floor. Other advantages of this include the promotion of muscle development in the neck and shoulders, and building up the muscles a baby needs to roll, sit and crawl.

A child who may begin to show signs of dyspraxia can only benefit from daily opportunities to develop these early skills, and early childhood settings are often the child's first community outside the home, so they are very influential in the identification of difficulties which the child may have been experiencing for some time.

Diagnosis

It is important that dyspraxia is diagnosed as early as possible, as children with motor difficulties are likely to be mislabelled as disruptive as their actions and behaviour can be misinterpreted by adults and other children. Frustration can lead to children becoming angry or withdrawn. What other children and adults see as thoughtless or clumsy actions may be out of the child's control, and causing them emotional distress which they cannot express effectively. They don't know

that they may have a developmental problem as this is their life, their experience, their reality day to day. If this can be prevented by the early signs being observed and acted upon in the early years' setting where there is an understanding of child growth and development, the long term looks far more positive.

When a child is observed with immaturities in planning and organising movement, or with problems associated with speech and language over a period of time, it is important that this is investigated.

GPs routinely see pre-school children whose development is causing concern. If this is then justified, the child can be referred to NHS therapy services, although this will vary from authority to authority. However, sound assessment of young children can be challenging because progress is uneven.

The Dyspraxia Foundation commissioned a parent survey (see resources section) which identified some disturbing issues:

• 65.4% of parents recognized that there was a problem with their child before they reached the age of three, but this was not picked up or commented upon during the developmental or pre-school review.

• Parents are most likely (25%) to consider first that their child might be dyspraxic. Only 9.4% of teachers and 1.8 % of GPs are likely to consider this diagnosis.

• Only 25% of dyspraxic children are recognized as such when they begin school and in 80% of cases schools think the child will 'grow out of it'.

• Over half of schools think that children with dyspraxia are naughty. This would appear to be based on a lack of awareness of the dyspraxic child's difficulty in following instructions and interpreting subtle messages and rules.

• Diagnosis is vital to the child's emotional well-being.

- Some families have had a long and difficult battle to achieve recognition of their child's difficulties.

Neuro-Developmental Delay

The Institute of Neuro-Physiological Psychology (INPP) has been the pioneer of work in the area of neuro-developmental delay (NDD) since 1975. Peter Blythe, founder of INPP, has been researching NDD since 1969 and he established INPP to investigate the links between physical development and problems with reading, writing, spelling, coordination, behaviour and emotional functioning in both adults and children. Sally Goddard-Blythe is currently Director of INPP and runs INPP's international training division. Both have published extensively and worked with thousands of children and families as well as developing a programme which is in use by teachers all over the world. By recognizing the fundamental importance of movement, they have campaigned passionately for an education system which is based on the crucial development in children of:

- Attention
- Balance
- Coordination

These are seen as the 'primary ABC' on which all later learning depends.

> The term NDD or Neuro-Developmental Delay describes the omission or arrest of a stage of early development. Every normal, full-term baby is born with a set of primitive or survival reflexes that are inhibited or controlled by higher centres in the brain during the first year of life. An infant does not have to think about making these movements, they occur automatically and without conscious thought. Generally, newborns will show strong reflexes around birth and these reflexes then tend to wane as the postural reflexes or gravity reflexes develop.

> If these are not inhibited at the correct time, they remain active in the body and can interfere with balance, motor control, eye functioning, eye-hand coordination and perceptual skills. They can result in behavioural symptoms such as frustration, hyperactivity and hypersensitivity, and failure to match performance to ability. (The Institute of Neuro-Physiological Psychology website www.inpp.org.uk).

Children need good quality movement experiences to help them to control and organize their voluntary movement and the speed at which this occurs is entirely individual. The brains of some children will mature quickly and efficiently in areas related to movement, but this is not the case for all children and for some, it will be a much slower process. In these cases, it is possible that primitive reflexes are undermining their ability to develop and a brief explanation of reflex inhibition and development may be useful at this point.

The Role of Reflexes

Primitive reflexes are inhibited by the developing brain during the first year of life and are gradually replaced by postural reflexes which develop in the first 3½ years of life to provide the basis for automatic (unconscious) control of balance, posture and voluntary movement. It is an accepted medical fact that retained primitive reflexes beyond the first 6–12 months of post-natal life indicate immaturity in the functioning of the Central Nervous System. This means that reflexes can be used by professionals as indicators that the system is not developing in an appropriate manner, either by a postural reflex not emerging, or through the continued presence of a primitive reflex after it should have been inhibited. This can happen for a number of reasons related to pregnancy, the birth process or even in early infancy.

If the transition from primitive to postural reflex is not completed in the first 3½ years of life, the child may experience problems with balance and coordination. Retained rooting and sucking reflexes, for example, can interfere with the development of clear speech as control of the muscles at the front of the mouth are affected and tongue position and swallow pattern remain immature. This can be seen in the child who is also a messy eater. The symmetrical tonic neck reflex affects coordination between the upper and lower halves of the body, is associated with poor muscle tone and can often be seen in the child who has poor sitting posture and who tends to slump on the desk when writing.

As the development of motor skills is such a crucial part of a child's development, any difficulties will have an impact on day to day living and have a wider effect on other areas of the child's development. Crawling, for example, has often been raised as important to later development and this brings us back to the opportunities babies have for exploration on the floor. The following quote from Chambers and Sugden neatly summarizes the issue:

> One must not think that just because a baby does not creep there is something wrong and it is indicative of impaired development in functions such as visual, cognitive or further motor skills … However, there are on-going investigations looking retrospectively at children who are later diagnosed as having DCD. Preliminary reports suggest that there is a higher incidence of non-creepers and non-crawlers in a DCD group than in matched non-DCD peers. (Chambers and Sugden (2006) *Early Years Movement Skills*).

What Are the Early Indicators of Dyspraxia?

Parents will often be aware of problems from an early age, either because of their experience with older siblings or because they 'just know', or other family members make comments. One of the difficulties with the early identification of dyspraxia may also be that parental concerns are not taken seriously by some health professionals and there are frustrating delays.

Practitioners can play a crucial role in the identification of difficulties if they are alert to early indicators.

In babies

A child's purposeful control over his body develops from top to bottom, so that the ability to move the head comes most easily then progresses down to the feet. It also develops from the inside to the outside: from the trunk outwards. Babies learn to lift and control their heads long before they can control their lower body well enough for balancing upright. They will also develop control from the midline of the body outwards so that control develops first in the shoulders and gradually outwards to the hands and fingers. Movement also becomes more precise as babies move from grasping toys with the whole hand to using a variety of hand positions and finger patterns to manipulate objects more purposefully.

Typically developing children are born hard-wired to master their body and they have an inner drive to challenge their balance skills and strength. They will repeat the same activities as they become increasingly self-confident and if they derive positive feedback from adults around them.

However, parents may have concerns about their child's development from a very early age if their child appears to be delayed, disorganized, underactive, passive and showing a tendency to avoid challenging circumstances.

In children aged birth to three

By the age of three, many of the symptoms of dyspraxia are often apparent.

Madeleine Portwood identifies a list of behaviours associated with dyspraxia which emerge from birth onwards and include:

- Feeding problems: fussy about texture of food and messy eater and poor weight gain

- Poor sleeping patterns

- Delayed early development: sitting, rolling and not going through a stage of crawling

- Sensitivity to high levels of noise or changes in light intensity

- Problems with toilet training

- Delayed language development

- Easily upset

- Weak concentration

- Parents notice that there is something 'different' with their child

- Frequently trips when running

- Difficulty sitting on a chair

- Unable to hop on one foot

- Holds crayon in fist

Other indicators include:

- Difficulty nursing/bottle drinking in infancy

- Difficulty imitating funny faces or mouth games

- Irritability

- Bouts of sickness and extreme colic

Speech Disorders

To be able to speak clearly, complex movements involving the tongue, lips, jaw and other structures need to be functioning efficiently. This means that many children with coordination problems will also have difficulty coordinating the movements needed to speak clearly.

- Difficulty nursing/ bottle drinking in infancy

- Open mouth posture, even without a stuffy nose

- Excessive drooling

- Tongue protruding

- Poor speech intelligibility

- Difficulty imitating funny faces or mouth games

- Limited ability to show emotion in facial expression

- Strong food preferences, slow to finish a meal

- Overstuffing food in the mouth

- Swallowing without chewing

- Grinding teeth

Parents are often made to feel that they are worrying unnecessarily and their insights into their child's struggles are dismissed as they are advised that their child will 'catch up' in their own time. It is only when the child transfers to an early years' setting that that their concerns will be taken more seriously by staff who are experts in child observation. The exposure to structured and unstructured activities make the difficulties more obvious to identify, as well as providing opportunities to observe the child interacting with others of a similar age.

In two to seven-year-olds

In the period from two to seven years of age children should be acquiring many movement skills which form the foundation of movements they will use throughout life. The rate and timings of individual progress depends on their own unique rate of development within broadly defined time-scales and is dependent on environmental, cultural and genetic factors. However, there are well-established milestones which are indicators of developmental status and which can be used to support concerns about a child's level of functioning and which can alert practitioners to the possibility of a child showing signs of dyspraxia. By the time they are five, or six, or seven, most children can run and jump, climb and swing and ride a bicycle. MacIntyre points out that these activities require a sophisticated sense of balance, coordination and control alongside feelings of achievement and satisfaction. If a child is experiencing the difficulties below, they are likely to be excluded from games and group activities and the social interaction that this involves.

Gross motor skills such as:

The child may be experiencing difficulties with a combination of these skills and this may vary according to time of day and circumstance.

- Tripping when running, an awkward running style

- Difficulty judging speed: how fast am I travelling?

- Difficulties judging distance: how far away or close are other people or objects?

- Balancing

- Jumping

- Hopping

- Skipping

- Climbing

- Ball skills: throwing a ball with direction

- Catching a 12' ball at age four

- Lack of rhythm and a tendency to be physically awkward

- Awkward walking on stairs

- Difficulties in PE and with apparatus

Fine motor skills such as:

- Making marks on paper

- Cutting with scissors

- Making models

- Clumsy when manipulating toys

- Very immature art work

Are there signs of ...?

- Poor spatial organization: Rosie may bump into other children or objects as she has difficulty judging distances accurately

- Sensitivity to noisy environments

- Difficulties in getting dressed and undressed

- Difficulties with eating skills

- Easily distracted by everyday sensory stimulation such as interactive whiteboards or lively wall displays

- Poor attention span

- Poor articulation: speech may be muddled

- Easily confused

- Anxious, excitable and easily distracted

- Poor social skills: a child who has a problem controlling his own body may often have difficulty reading the body language of others and will not realize or respond to these cues. As a result, they may become unpopular as other children cannot understand their behaviour

Any delay in the acquisition of these skills can lead to children like Rosie losing their self-confidence, developing behaviour and concentration problems, and becoming the distractible child who can never sit still.

If a child is also criticized for patterns of behaviour which they have no control over, frustration and poor behaviour are likely to become a feature of their daily functioning. Girls have also been noted to have a tendency to withdraw into themselves as they become frustrated. Staff need to be alert to the child who seems almost invisible during the day.

Age seven upwards

The longer the dyspraxic child goes without being identified, the greater the experience of frustration, failure and anxiety. Liam becomes used to what feels like daily criticism and humiliation and he learns not to expect too much from experiences in school and in the playground.

Although many 'normal children' will show some of the signs below, for children like Liam, these will be severe, on-going and evident in many different situations.

- Persistence of pre-school problems with little or no improvement e.g. difficulties with fastenings on clothing

- Avoidance of physical activity and organized PE: team games are an issue

- Poor attention span and ability to follow verbal instructions

- Inability to complete written work at the expected speed and with appropriate presentation

- Copying down information and poor handwriting

- Reading, spelling and maths activities can cause anxiety

- The child may seem disorganized as more is expected of them

- Poor speech production

- Lack of confidence

- Friendship issues

- Emotional outbursts/ over-reactions

- Behavioural problems

- Poor social skills and often lack of awareness of 'unwritten' and subtle social rules

Tips for supporting children in Key Stage 2 and beyond with Dyspraxia

- Have consistent, structured routines which have been negotiated. For example: have a designated routine for getting ready for school and for preparing and emptying the school bag. Use daily timetables

- Work closely with parents so that there are common expectations and understandings

- Experiment with samples of different types of pens and pencils in stationery shops. Retractable pencils are good for older pupils as they can help them regulate how much pressure they are using

- Plan ahead for activities such as swimming so that Liam can practise getting used to changing, using lockers and, if possible, learn to swim competently outside of school

- Make sure that everything for school is where it needs to be and that you have doubles of resources such as pencils, cases: one at school and one at home

- Ensure that personnel at the school and any activity clubs etc. are aware of the child's difficulties so that they can anticipate problems and short circuit them if necessary

- Recognize the difficulties and that the child is struggling by providing encouragement and telling him that you know he is not being lazy

- Look at ways to help him relax: a CD such as The Imagination Gym (see resources) has been used very successfully with children who need to learn to relax to a guided visualization

- Provide a quiet working place without distractions such as television

This has been adapted from some of the indicators identified by Lois Addy in her book: *How to understand and support children with Dyspraxia* (LDA 2004).

Case study – Callum

Callum is learning to dress himself. He is three years old. His early life experiences have not always been positive either for him or for his parents and other family members. Callum is the third of four children, and his parents felt right from early on that he was not following in the footsteps of his brothers and sisters. A poor feeder and sleeper, Callum often seemed 'floppy' as a baby and his parents didn't have an unbroken night's sleep until he was aged two and a half. He did eventually crawl, and he seemed to be a bright boy, interacting well with others but with some speech delay.

Callum's parents expressed their concerns to their GP when he was two, and they were advised to keep an eye on his progress, but not to be overly concerned but they still know that he needs a much higher level of care than his brothers or sisters. The GP thinks they are being over-protective and over-anxious.

Family gatherings are also difficult as Callum doesn't play with other children very well and his clumsiness marks him out. They don't know how to explain his difficulties to family and friends as there is nothing obviously 'wrong' with him. His mother is often embarrassed by the way he manages food and drink when she compares him to cousins of a similar age.

The health visitor has helped his parents with ideas and suggestions and she agrees that Callum may be showing early signs of developmental coordination difficulties.

One of the suggestions made for the parents and setting to work on with Callum related to strategies for developing self-help skills in general, and getting dressed in particular. A visual prompt was suggested as well as a sticker chart for positive praise.

Callum's getting dressed routine:

First the pants, then the tracksuit bottoms, making sure that they are the right way round and that one foot goes in each leg of the tracksuit. Next the vest, not inside out and back to front. Then the t-shirt, pulling it over his head. He is asked to lift his arms as he needs some help for this. After that, Callum needs reminding to sit down and to lean forward to pull on his socks. This can be very frustrating as they wrinkle and the heel of the sock is on the wrong side, and sometimes his toes get caught. By the time Callum's shoes are on, he's often in tears as getting dressed is always a battle with sequencing, balance, gravity and manipulation skills.

Now he's ready for nursery, and it's into the buggy: walking with Callum takes way too long as he often seems to have two left feet and his mother needs to get to work on time. At nursery, Callum will need prompting to go to the toilet and he may be unable to coordinate pulling down his trousers, using the toilet and toilet paper. As a result, accidents happen and his parents are used to taking him home in a different set of clothes. The nursery staff are now working to an Individual Education Plan with Callum and developing better self-help skills has been identified as one key target for Callum. His parents have shared their concerns with the nursery right from the start and they were relieved when this was taken seriously. Callum's key person, Tasha, lets them know how Callum is getting on and she makes a point of telling the parents positive news about Callum when he is being collected. Tasha has a visual timetable which she can use to remind Callum of what will be happening during the day, including when he will have a drink and snack. She has used a digital camera to take a series of photos of Callum. These are then laminated and Velcro is stuck on the back so that each day can be personalized for him on the chart that she has prepared. This can then be shared with Callum at various points of the day. The photos can be moved around depending on the activities Callum choses, as this then can act as a record of what he has done.

The key person has shared this idea with his parents who are now beginning to use it at home as well to help Callum remember the order of things to do.

Case study – Liam

Liam is struggling in his class. He does not have effective systems which enable him to process events going on around him, to ignore sounds in the background and so he is often in trouble for lack of concentration and attention. His teacher reports that he has a poor attention span, although he works well on a one to one basis. Fidgety children are sometimes seen as affecting the development of those around them, and their behaviour can be attributed to poor parenting or to a disruptive personality.

Liam has a history of excitability and overreacts to classroom events around him. His clumsy movements and speech difficulties are the source of teasing and Liam has been known to react emotionally to the extent that he has been excluded from school on several occasions. Liam just thinks it's not fair that everyone picks on him.

Liam's mother is very worried about him and feels that whatever she does, nothing gets any better for Liam. She worries that he may not only have dyspraxia, but also ADHD, and that the situation will continue to deteriorate if steps are not taken to prevent Liam's increasing frustration, anxiety and social isolation. She worries that he is trying to buy friendship and that he is clowning around in class to get acceptance from other pupils. He does not have friends and is relatively isolated outside school. He gets upset and tells her often that he has been told off for poor handwriting and for dropping his books.

He is always the last to be chosen as a partner or team member. His teacher is frustrated by his behaviour and has noticed that he frequently asks to go to the toilet as a work avoidance tactic.

A new SENCO at the school has helped Liam's mother to put down her concerns on paper and to compile a list of observed difficulties both at school and at home. This report is now being used to prepare an Individual Education Plan in consultation with Liam himself. His mother will also use the report to approach her GP again for referral for a formal assessment of Liam's difficulties.

Liam has now been selected to join a movement class after school. This is run by a teacher who has been trained by The Institute of Neuro-Physiological Psychology (INPP) in the use of the INPP Schools' Programme. The programme is based on a growing body of evidence to support the long-held theory that control of balance, motor skills and integration of early reflexes are linked to academic achievement. If a cluster of abnormal primitive and postural reflexes is present, it will interfere with the development of control of balance and motor skills. A reflex stimulation and inhibition programme can help to provide a solid foundation for the improvement of motor skills, and thereby improve balance, coordination and confidence.

These problems can be identified by trained teachers, and a series of studies over the last five years demonstrates that, in many cases, something can be done about them. The remedy is a simple daily exercise programme, which can be carried out in school for ten minutes per day. This programme is devised by INPP and is based on a clinical programme that has been in use since the 1970s.

Liam enjoys the programme because the movements are easy to do and no-one makes fun of him. The teacher has also been given some funding so that they can work on decent mats and they get a drink and some fruit as well. His teacher will work with the children on the programme for approximately one year and they will be assessed for progress across a number of areas such as balance, coordination, literacy skills and handwriting.

How Can the Setting Support the Child?

Most children in pre-school with coordination difficulties are unlikely to have a diagnosis of dyspraxia as it is difficult to distinguish between dyspraxia and developmental delay at this early age. There may be a number of reasons why a child's motor skills appear to be delayed and these may improve with age and with increased opportunities to develop these skills in a range of activities.

Some children with coordination difficulties may be very unsettled by the changes in their routine that take place when they begin to attend the setting and they will need careful support to help them feel secure.

Children with Developmental Coordination Disorder (DCD) lack the motor coordination necessary to perform tasks considered appropriate for their age, given normal intellectual ability and the absence of other neurological disorders.

This means that movements, from the simple to the complex, will need to be built carefully so that firm foundations for later learning can take place. Just as in building a house: there's no point working on the bedrooms if the foundations are shaky!

We need to offer challenges that are equal to the skills the child currently possesses; otherwise we are setting them up for failure, anxiety and an expectation that they will fail when faced with new experiences.

As the extent of the overlap and co-existence of developmental disorders begins to unfold, it becomes clear that there should be a greater emphasis on the importance of motor skills and developing competent movement patterns from the earliest days. The period of two to seven years of age is one of great change and there is an expectation that children will be developing good body control which supports their independence in play situations, self-help and social interaction. This means that children need wide and varied opportunities to develop body control for skills such as:

- Running

- Jumping

- Skipping

- Climbing

- Rolling

- Crawling

- Catching and throwing

- Balancing

- Eating

- Manipulating toys and mark making

Many children have poor quality of movement as a key element in their need for additional support. This means that it is important that a high value is placed on providing a setting which is rich in movement activities linked to other aspects of learning. Even with children with no specific 'label', movement is being found to be linked to learning, and educational professionals need to be confident in knowing how to support children who continue not to meet their motor milestones at the expected time.

Informal Assessment

At the initial stages, you may want to observe the child on a number of occasions with a particular focus in mind. You will of course be speaking to other practitioners, the SENCO and to the child's parents to develop a broader perspective of the difficulties and also, importantly, areas of strength.

Find out about the support your SENCO can give you in relation to the setting's SEN (Special Educational Needs) policy and how you can access support from an outside specialist.

Children do things differently on different occasions depending on the time of day, whether they are tired, and many other factors. As a result, a series of observations is more likely to provide the evidence of the level of a child's movement difficulties. As their patterns of behaviour and movement can be variable, Macintyre recommends, for example, checking that other aspects of the child's development are not affecting performance such as poor vision or hearing loss. This is an important point as practitioners may not always be immediately aware (or have been told) of sight, hearing or speech difficulties which may result in slower responses which are then misinterpreted as signs of dyspraxia.

Children born with poor sight or hearing, may not even realize that they have an impairment. If they are used to following what others are doing around them their responses may be inaccurate or late, depending on whether the signals they are copying are themselves accurate or appropriate.

When you observe dyspraxic children closely, you may see that many of their difficulties appear to relate to working out how to carry out the movements they need to make in the appropriate sequence. As they hesitate, they may become fearful or anxious and become confused as they fail to complete the activity with success.

You may observe dyspraxic children engaging in 'mirror' movements. This means that parts of their body which are not directly involved in the activity also move. For example, when jumping or hopping they may use their arms unusually or when the right hand is doing something, the left hand is 'mirroring' the action. When sitting down, and playing at a table, the child's legs and feet may be tapping or swinging at the same time.

Talk to the child's parent(s) or carer(s) about the child's early development. The indicators of dyspraxia in babies can form a useful starting point. It is important to be sensitive to the way in which parents are approached about this as they may be unable or unwilling to discuss early parenting experiences if they feel they are being criticized.

Some parents may already be feeling some guilt or lack of confidence in how they have managed these early experiences. If you approach this with sensitivity and with an understanding of the basics of dyspraxia and its implications, you will have a good foundation to build on.

Infants, Movement and Learning

Over the years, researchers have looked into the relationship between movements that infants make and their developing minds. The importance of understanding the ways in which motor development takes place is linked to our understanding of how infants learn and develop in other ways. Since motor development generally occurs in a predictable order in typically developing infants, it can be used to recognize when an infant is not following this predictable pattern. The developmental milestones which parents and health professionals refer to are well-established: these are landmarks or turning points in an individual's development and are linked to one another in a relatively consistent sequence.

However, there are a number of factors which can influence when these developmental markers are reached. A cultural phenomenon identified in the United States is 'first child syndrome' where first time mothers may hold their infants for long periods and avoid putting them on their stomachs for a long time. There is the suggestion that these periods of prolonged holding result in the delayed onset of certain motor milestones such as crawling, as the infant is not given opportunities to strengthen neck muscles when lying prone (on their stomachs).

From this we can see that the development of movement skill may be influenced by:

- The parents' confidence and experience of handing infants

- Parental expectations of the infant

- The environment the infant is brought up in

- The infant's genetic temperament

- The infant's profile of development

Health professionals will be familiar with typical developmental milestones such as those above it is recognized that there is wide variability in the development of each individual child, but there is a predictability in typical development which allows us to predict that development is delayed or advanced compared to other children. When a child's development differs from the norm, there may or may not be a cause for concern.

Balance

Balance affects everything a child tries to do. It is a significant ability in all aspects of movement, and standing still is one of the most difficult things we can ask a child to do.

Macintyre points out that some children will find it difficult to maintain static balance (maintaining balance and poise when the body is still), because they may have retained primitive reflexes which are causing them to react in an involuntary manner when

in certain positions. Children who have a reduced sense of where they are in space will have difficulties balancing and in planning and organizing their movements such as sitting, standing and climbing.

Sally Goddard-Blythe's book, *The Well-Balanced Child* (Movement and Early Learning, 2007), is an excellent source of information in this field. She puts forward a passionate manifesto for a 'whole body' approach to learning which integrates the brain, senses, movement and play.

Windows of Achievement for six gross motor milestones

Sitting without support	4–9 months
Crawling on hands and knees	6–10 months
Standing with assistance	5–11 months
Walking with assistance	6–14 months
Standing alone	6.5–17 months
Walking alone	8–18 months

Source: World Health Organization Multicentre Growth Reference Study Group 2006

Other Milestones

Running	A child usually runs safely by 24 months and well by 30 months
Jumping	At 30 months a child can usually jump from a low step
Hopping	Achieved by four years
Climbing stairs	The child will go upstairs one foot after the other at three years and come down stairs one foot after the other at four years
Riding a tricycle/bicycle	A child usually begins to pedal at two years of age and many children begin to ride a bicycle without stabilizers from five or six years of age
Skipping	This is usually achieved by age five
Standing on one leg	Most children can stand momentarily on one leg at age three. By four years this lasts for three to five seconds and by five years for eight to ten seconds
Throwing and catching balls	At three years of age a child can throw a ball overhand and catch a large ball between extended arms. By four years they can use a bat

Source: World Health Organization Multicentre Growth Reference Study Group 2006

Practical Suggestions

When a child has a movement difficulty, they will need practice in planning their movements, in copying others and in predicting what to do and how to do it. This may mean going back to very simple movements and providing daily opportunities for successful completion of activities which have been identified as relevant.

Instructions

Give clear simple instructions, having gained the child's attention by using his name.

Use your voice as a tool: If you want the child to move slowly, speak slowly. If you want them to move quietly, speak quietly: children will more often react positively to a quiet voice than someone shouting or with a raised voice. For minor problems, ignore the behaviour until it stops and then immediately praise any positive behaviour.

Be:

• Consistent: stay calm, acknowledge when a child has difficulties and help them to find ways to achieve what they are trying to do. Consistent routines and instructions help children to develop security, so that they feel confident to take risks.

• Honest: focus on the behaviour of the child more than the quality of their performance: 'I like the way you tried to do the puzzle: it's a bit hard isn't it? You did a good job!'

• Sincere: even young children know if you are praising them for something which is not actually good. Insincerity helps no-one and can make the child distrust you. Honest, but thoughtful comments can help a child to grow in confidence as can positive focused praise such as: 'Rosie, I like the way you shared with Callum'.

• Explicit: it helps if you state your expectations clearly and in terms that the child can understand. This may need to involve visual aids such as a visual timetable or signing if necessary. 'Can you put the puzzle back in the tray? That's so good, now it's all tidy again...'

Routines

Starting at nursery can be difficult for many children. Whereas some will be able to adapt to new routines and surroundings, others can find this emotionally upsetting. As an early years setting, you will have routines and structures in place, but these may need to be adapted for individual children and explained in advance if possible.

Toilets

Help may be needed with toilet routines and with general use of the toilet and sink. Remember that the planning and coordination of movements is difficult for some children.

Think about whether the routines of your setting are making life difficult for Rosie. Are the routines flexible enough for her to take the time she might need on her activity or for eating or getting dressed? Do you need to consider changing or adapting your planning?

Practice, Practice, Practice

Opportunities to practise or rehearse new skills allow these to become automatic so that children are not aware that they are being performed competently. Some children make progress and learn very quickly whilst others, with more challenges to overcome, will need far more repetition in order to establish automatic competence.

Model and practice games and role play where there is turn taking and cooperation. Talk about what you are doing: 'I am sharing this toy with Rochelle because she likes to play with it. Do you like this toy too?'

Provide sequencing games such as jumping from one carpet tile to another in different patterns. Model this first, and sometimes pretend to get it wrong.

Adapt all activities, progressing from simple to more complex in different contexts.

Rhythm Activities

Clapping activities can demonstrate the rhythm of words as can using a drum or similar instrument when moving.

Praise

Use positive, focused praise: 'Rosie, I really liked it when you shared that with Callum.'

Modeling Activities to Support Learning

Young children learn from copying and so, by providing a role model, you help them to understand and learn more readily. This also helps to get over the message without relying only on giving verbal instructions. Children are always watching you and everything you do potentially teaches them a lesson. If we want our children to be confident, polite and sociable, we need to demonstrate those behaviours consistently.

At the same time, using key words regularly helps the child to develop language and sequencing skills.

Generally children master gross motor skills such as catching or kicking a ball before fine motor skills. Children with dyspraxia tend to have difficulty across the whole range of motor skills, although some will develop competent fine motor skills, but have difficulty with the gross motor skills they need to be able to cope with physical activities involving movement and space.

Gross Motor Skills

Gross motor skills are the movements of the large muscles of the body. Gross motor skills include:

- Balance – the ability to maintain equilibrium in different positions

- Body awareness – for improved posture and control

- Crossing of the mid-line – this is the ability to cross our right side over to our left and vice versa. You might observe a child painting on the right side of the paper with their right hand and then swapping to the left hand for the left side of the paper

- Laterality – awareness of the left and right sides of the body

- Spatial orientation – awareness of the body position in space and in relation to other objects or people

Without reasonable gross motor skills, children often struggle with the fine motor skills that are required for formal school work.

In the setting, the children will need access to equipment and activities which can sensitively be differentiated to adapt to individual needs and challenges.

Fine Motor Skills

Most children will have developed a hand preference by 30 months, but this is not always the case (Tassoni P (2008), *The Practical EYFS Handbook*. Heinemann). There should be plenty of opportunities to carry out activities using both hands. One important factor in developing fine motor control is the provision of varying activities that interest the child and encourage them. Children's hands are more sensitive than adults and this may affect how they feel about handling some textures.

Tassoni suggests that these children need more exposure to such sensory activities to help them become slowly desensitized. Using a barrier such as a clear bag or see through gloves can help in this respect as well as providing a bowl of water so that they can wash their hands at any point if they feel the need to.

Art Activities

Children with dyspraxia will need regular practice of activities to improve their fine motor skills. Experiment with different types of brushes and other resources, bearing in mind that some children do not like the feeling of paint on their fingers or they may dislike the smell of what you are using. If a child seems reluctant to participate in these activities, consider how this can be adapted so that they can build up a better tolerance

The following will help to develop strength in fingers and the ability to manipulate objects for a purpose.

- Squeezy toys in water

- Washing-up liquid bottles

- Natural sponges

- Thick board markers

- Pencils in damp sand

- Shallow trays with washable paint and a bowl of water to rinse hands afterwards

- Paper stuck to wall with masking tape

Construction Toys

Children may have difficulty with the handling of parts of jigsaws or construction toys. They may not be able to work out which way round they should go or how to fit pieces together as the ability to hold the pieces and to move them around depends on the ability to grip and rotate objects. Chunky toys and pieces which fit together with minimum effort will help build confidence and success.

Posture is also important as Rosie may need to be helped to find a stable sitting position so that she can concentrate on what she is doing.

Bubbles, whistles, bendy straws

These can be used to strengthen and improve the coordination of the lips and mouth.

Social Skills

Group Activities

You may observe Rosie standing too close to other children or showing frustration if she is aware that she cannot carry out activities as the same level as others in the group. She may want to watch rather than participate.

Self Care Skills

Children have variable levels of motivation to develop self-care independence. She suggests selecting goals that are driven by the child's interests and motivation. When 'catching' a child trying to do something independently reinforce the positive behaviour with rewards. By cutting down the number of steps in any task as far as possible and helping the child by providing picture charts to help them remember the steps they need to follow.

Eating

Eating and drinking can be a tricky area, full of potential hazards and a cause of anxiety and stress.

Having been a faddy baby, Rosie may not be able to tolerate some textures of food and she will avoid them if possible and they may make her feel physically sick. Carers can provide vital information about this.

She will need a cup and cutlery which she can handle easily and some food which can be eaten with her fingers. These skills can be practised in play activities as well to help Rosie develop the skills she will need as she progresses to greater self-help and independence.

A damp face-cloth or baby wipe can be used in front of a mirror to develop an understanding of cleaning up if they are having problems with the mechanics of getting food into their mouths.

Dressing up Games

Dressing and dressing up can be a source of frustration for children who struggle with buttons, fastenings, zips etc. By sitting on the floor, with their back against a wall, they can balance more easily and feel steadier.

They may feel more motivated if they have a choice of clothes as well which will be easier to put on if they are slightly oversized.

Key Points

- Dyspraxic children need more time. Don't rush them or do the task for them. They do need to develop independence, not what is called 'learned helplessness', where they have come to expect someone else to do things for them.

- Use routines to support them in predicting and anticipating.

- Physical skills must be broken down into simple parts and taught. They will not develop on their own. These then need daily practice.

- Recording progress using stickers/charts/photos can help reinforce that progress is indeed taking place. This means that the child is competing against themselves rather than against an age-related target. Performance may only improve very gradually and this should not be compared to other children's achievement.

- Encourage carers to dress the child in clothes which minimize difficulties and length of time needed to get dressed or go to the toilet.

- Let the child know that you realize some things are difficult for them, but that does not mean they are stupid. Use positive feedback: 'Well done Jay: you carried that really well!'

- Agree with carers how to share information about dyspraxia with other parents of children in the setting to help them develop some understanding of why children may be behaving in a certain way.

- Practice is important when learning new skills. It helps children to make sense of their learning and strengthens brain connections.

How Can the Setting Support the Child's Carers?

Parents are notoriously excellent observers of their own child's strengths and weaknesses, even when they lack formal in training of what should be expected of a 'normally' developing child. Because parents see their child acting on a daily basis with other children, they are usually the first to observe that their child is more awkward than his or her peers. For this reason, unless the child has a specific medical condition that places him or her at risk for developmental delay, it is often the parent, and not a teacher or pediatrician, who first expresses concern about a child's development and ability to function.

It has always been good practice to involve carers and, by making sure that you include them in some of the decision-making such as planning and contributing to their child's records, you can begin to develop a more rounded picture of their child. Sharing information is particularly important when it is necessary to sensitively approach the subject of their child's progress.

Some questions you may be thinking about:

• What are the family's concerns?

• What routines can we discuss working on?

• What are the practical issues we can support the family with?

• What is important to Callum and his family?

• What action can we take when we observe Rosie struggling?

Some questions carers may be wanting to ask:

• How will I know that Rosie is OK?

• Should I tell other parents about her problems?

• What can I do if the doctor thinks I'm just fussing?

• Is it my fault Rosie is like this?

Sometimes carers may already feel that their concerns have not being taken seriously by other family members, the health visitor or the GP. They may already be looking to you for guidance and for recognition that they are right to be worried or concerned about their child's progress.

Feelings of guilt, that it is somehow their fault and that they have not been able to be a 'good' parent are often expressed. If they also feel that they have not been listened to, they may express frustration as they should be the person who knows the child best of all.

However, the child's carers may not recognize that there is anything out of the ordinary and this is where your discussions need to be supported by the evidence from your observations. It is essential to share your concerns with the carer and to offer a programme of activities or suggestions for ways to help at home as this is the best way to improve overall progress. Some carers may be in denial about any delay or difficulty and may not be ready to accept your advice.

Practical Suggestions for Carers

Hugs, care and love
If a child experiences hugs and love as a part of his daily life, they are more likely to be able to deal with his frustration. A child needs to know that he is valued by his carers and by those he comes into contact with (adults and children) in the setting. By recognizing that he is struggling with some aspects of daily living, you give the message that he is OK; 'I know that was a bit tricky wasn't it Callum? Shall we do it together?'

Focused Praise
Even with young children, it is important that they understand what they have done well. Instead of 'Good boy Callum', it is more effective to be clear about what he has done that is good: 'Well done Callum, look at how you put your t-shirt on all by yourself! Let's draw a smiley face on the chart.'

Time for Sharing
Children need adults who can find the time to listen to them and who are relaxed when playing with them. Slow motion games and 'statues' help to develop good control of movement.

Day to Day
Help carers to learn to accept that their child is going to need extra time to complete activities. This can be frustrating for adults if they have not anticipated this problem or have not had experience of this issue with their other children.

By building in plenty of time, patience and practice, combined with praise, progress will be made. Help carers to accept that their child's performance will also deteriorate under pressure. This will prepare them for the occasions when, as adults, they feel frustrated with the way in which their child is behaving.

Ask them to tell you in front of the child when they do reach a goal or begin to demonstrate a new skill at home. This reinforces your communication and adds to your records.

Dressing

Getting dressed is a complex activity which involves sequencing, balance, fine motor control, coordination and an understanding of concepts such as 'back', 'front', 'top' and 'next'. Sometimes it is seen as easier to dress the child, particularly when there are time pressures. However, carers can be helped to develop strategies to give their child independence and to prevent frustration and anger.

Variability

Children have 'good days' when they can do things better than on other days. This is particularly true of children with a dyspraxic profile. Adults need to remember this when the child's performance can be very different from one part of the day to another.

Toys, Equipment

Special toys, music and games to stimulate a child are great, but it is more important to share daily activities which carers can carry out with their child to encourage development.

Look at providing parents with activity cards they can use at home which use regular household resources rather than expensive toys which may not be appropriate.

Various types of pegs, for example can be used for sequencing, developing fine motor strength and control.

Simple puzzles, sorting games and ball games with a large soft ball are all useful basic resources which can be used to develop fine and gross motor skills.

Regardless of the activity, sensory activities are more effective when selected by the child and carried out as meaningful tasks, self-directed which capitalize on the child's inner drive.

Professional Support

Professional support can come from health visitors or GPs, if you know that they will be supportive. Health visitors are often an excellent source of good advice and can be a very useful local contact. For children in pre-school, the health visitor or general practitioner (GP) is often the first point of contact, leading to referral to child development specialists and onward referral to an occupational therapist and/or speech and language therapist. This will vary according to the local health authority and demand on services.

It's not possible to cure dyspraxia, but children can be taught strategies so they can achieve their full potential. This involves a team approach, using the skills of many different specialists such as occupational therapists, speech and language therapists, psychologists and specialist teachers. The programme will depend on the child's strengths and weaknesses and advice and exercises will generally be given to help the child and their family come to terms with the challenges dyspraxia can cause.

Rosie

Rosie didn't always want to go to nursery and she made it difficult for her mother by not cooperating in getting dressed. Her mother had given up trying to get her to eat in the morning as she wouldn't try most breakfast foods. She was still using a bottle as there had been so many accidents with cups, spilt milk and juice that this had become another battlefield.

Arriving at nursery, she used to be reluctant to leave her mother and there was a struggle to get her coat off as she would cling on and scream.

Later, on many mornings, when walking past a group of children at a table, she would knock over a paint pot, bump into another child and burst into tears with frustration.

What the setting did to help

What helped practitioners to raise concern, was that Rosie's clumsiness and poor gross motor skills were not mirrored in other areas of her development where she was making at least average progress.

Rosie's key worker approached her mother discreetly and suggested a short informal meeting to share some thoughts about how to make day to day living easier for Rosie both in the setting and at home.

The key worker and mother identified ways to help Rosie get ready in the morning and a visual timetable was developed which helped Rosie know what to expect.

A special photo diary was developed to share all the positive moments and strategies were talked through to help Rosie manage eating and drinking more independently.

Rosie's Foundation Stage Unit places a very high priority on developmental movement and on breaking down basic movement patterns into their simplest forms. The children are all encouraged to participate in activities such as crawling and rolling in lots of different ways so help them become very competent with these skills and a rich variety of sensory experiences are provided. Children also learn more about carrying out movements in a slow and controlled way which helps them improve their balance and control. All practitioners have attended training to support their continuing professional development in this area and they have hosted training for a cluster of schools using a programme called Move to Learn (see resources section).

Rosie will not grow out of her dyspraxia, but early intervention can help her to overcome her difficulties and, with support from the health visitor and her GP, Rosie has now been referred for assessment.

Last Words

Children need to experience successful movement in order to foster their development, to learn about themselves, how they interact with their environment and the constant adaptations they must make as it changes. The ability to move well is important in its own right and also because it permeates into other facets of the child's development, e.g. learning about themselves and how to cope in a changing, more demanding world.

'If you can't run fast enough, you don't get to play. It's not fair. It's really not fair!' Scott, aged 5 (The above quote is courtesy of Macintyre's excellent book: *Dyspraxia in the Early Years*).

What I hope is that this book might give you is some insight into how Scott is feeling and what you can do to help him grow, thrive and succeed. Persistence, patience and obstinacy are useful, if not essential characteristics which will be needed to ensure that Scott's needs are met as early as possible, that he is listened to and informed action is taken.

Resources

Addy L (2004) *How to understand and support children with Dyspraxia.* LDA, Cambridge

Boon M (2001) *Helping Children with Dyspraxia.* Jessica Kingsley Publishers, London

Chambers M, Sugden D (2006) *Early Movement Skills: Description, Diagnosis and Intervention.* Whurr Publishers, Chichester

Goddard-Blythe S (2008) *What Babies and Children Really Need.* Hawthorn Press, Stroud

Goddard-Blythe S (2007) *The Well-Balanced Child: Movement and Early Learning.* Hawthorn Press, Stroud

Macintyre C (2009) *Dyspraxia 5–11: A Practical Guide.* David Fulton Publishers, Oxon

Macintyre C (2009) *Dyspraxia in the Early Years.* David Fulton Publishers, Oxon

Tassoni P (2008) *Practical EYFS Handbook.* Heinemann, Essex

Sources of Information:

The Dyspraxia Foundation
www.dyspraxiafoundation.org.uk
The foundation offers a range of services, information and support. The Parental Survey referred to on page xx is available on this site.

The Institute for Neuro-Physiological Psychology
www.inpp.org.uk
INPP run training courses and their web-site has information about this as well as many other resources.

Move to Learn
www.movetolearn.com.au
Move to Learn provides a very useful questionnaire on-line to help identify the nature of their child's learning difficulties. It also has many resources such as books and training which are available from mem@imaginationgym.ws

Wolverhampton City NHS Speech and Language Therapy: Verbal Dyspraxia Information Leaflet for Parents and Teachers
This is available from the Speech and Language Therapy Services, The Gem Centre, Neachells Lane, Wednesfield, Wolverhampton, WV11 3PG

Other Related Resources

Screen Learning
www.smartcatlearning.com
This is an interactive website which enables parents and schools to access a suite of games which identify strengths and weaknesses in a child's learning profile, including dyslexia.

Imagination Gym: The Enchanted Forest
www.imaginationgym.ws
This is a lovely CD which I have used successfully with children who have problems with relaxing. With repeated use, the child can fully relax. This in turn helps to stimulate creativity, relaxation and fun, which enhance the overall learning process.

Mary Mountstephen can be contacted directly for further information and training for early years' settings, further education establishments and cluster groups.
mem@imaginationgym.ws